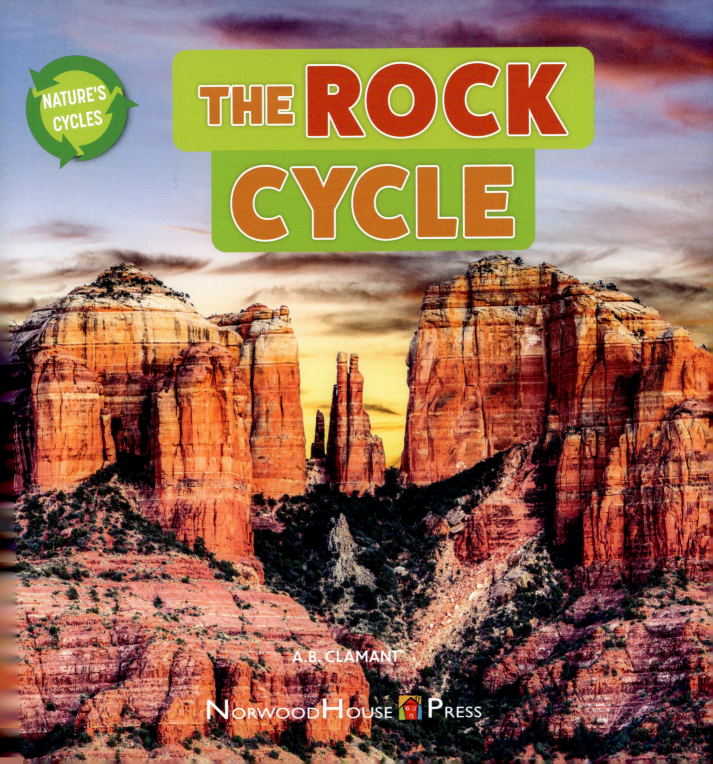

Cataloging-in-Publication Data

Names: Clamant, A.B., 1972-.
Title: The rock cycle / A.B. Clamant.
Description: Buffalo, NY : Norwood House Press, 2026. | Series: Nature's cycles | Includes glossary and index.
Identifiers: ISBN 9781978575677 (pbk.) | ISBN 9781978575684 (library bound) | ISBN 9781978575691 (ebook)
Subjects: LCSH: Geochemical cycles--Juvenile literature. | Petrology--Juvenile literature.
Classification: LCC QE432.2 C536 2026 | DDC 552'.06--dc23

Published in 2026 by
Norwood House Press
2544 Clinton Street
Buffalo, NY 14224

Copyright © 2026 Norwood House Press
Designer: Rhea Magaro
Editor: Kim Thompson

Photo credits: Cover, p. 1 Sean Pavone/Shutterstock.com; p. 3 NatalyFox/Shutterstock.com; p. 5 BlueRingMedia/Shutterstock.com; p. 6 Yngstrom/Shutterstock.com; p. 7 Martin Korsawe/Shutterstock.com; p. 9 jessicahyde/Shutterstock.com; p. 10 Copter Ural/Shutterstock.com; p. 11 Paul B. Moore/Shutterstock.com; p. 12 Forsal3/Shutterstock.com; p. 13 Piotr Velixar/Shutterstock.com; p. 15 Jane Rix/Shutterstock.com; p. 16 Amit kg/Shutterstock.com; p. 17 Sam Trench/Shutterstock.com; p. 18 U.S Geological Survey/Shutterstock.com; p. 19 Pung/Shutterstock.com; p. 21 Sophon Nawit /Shutterstock.com

All rights reserved. No part of this book may be reproduced in any form without permission in writing from the publisher, except by a reviewer.

Printed in the United States of America

Some of the images in this book illustrate individuals who are models. The depictions do not imply actual situations or events.

CPSIA compliance information: Batch #CSNHP26: For further information contact Norwood House Press at 1-800-237-9832.

TABLE OF CONTENTS

What Is the Rock Cycle? 4

Igneous Rock Forms 6

Sedimentary Rock Forms 8

Metamorphic Rock Forms 14

The Cycle Continues 18

Glossary 22

Thinking Questions 23

Index 24

About the Author 24

What Is the Rock Cycle?

Pick up a stone from the ground. Do you know where it came from? Did you know that rocks move around Earth over time? All rocks are part of the rock **cycle**.

Igneous Rock Forms

The rock cycle begins deep below Earth's surface. There, hot **magma** flows.

When a volcano erupts, magma shoots out. Once magma is on Earth's surface, it is called lava. When lava cools, it hardens into rock. This kind of rock is **igneous** rock.

Sedimentary Rock Forms

Over time, igneous rocks change. Water, wind, and ice wear them down. Cracks form. Bits break off. This is called **weathering**.

The loose bits of rock get carried away. They get swept along by moving water. They get blown by the wind. They are taken to new places. This is called **erosion**.

The Grand Canyon is an example of erosion. The Colorado River has worn away the rock for at least five million years!

The bits of rock that get carried away by erosion are called **sediment**. Sediment collects at the bottom of rivers, lakes, and oceans.

Sediment mixes with **silt**, clay, and other rocks. Over time, many layers of sediment form. The sediment in the bottom layers gets pushed and squeezed together. It becomes **sedimentary** rock.

13

Metamorphic Rock Forms

Sedimentary rocks get pushed deeper and deeper under Earth's surface. They heat up.

Heat and pressure can change sedimentary rock into **metamorphic** rock. This can also happen to igneous rocks that get pushed under Earth's surface.

The **minerals** in metamorphic rock change, or morph. Heat and pressure squeeze and fold the rocks. This gives them a new shape.

The Cycle Continues

Over time, metamorphic rocks get pushed deeper into Earth. They are under even more pressure. They get hotter.

When metamorphic rock gets hot enough, it melts. It turns into magma. The rock cycle starts all over again.

19

The next time you pick up a rock, remember its journey through the rock cycle. It has been moving and changing for hundreds of millions of years!

Glossary

cycle (SYE-kuhl): a series of events that repeat over and over in the same order

erosion (i-ROH-zhuhn): the process by which bits of rock are carried away by wind, water, or ice

igneous (ig-NEE-uhs): related to rocks that form when a volcano erupts; obsidian and pumice are examples of igneous rocks

magma (MAG-muh): melted rock below Earth's surface

metamorphic (met-uh-MOR-fik): related to rocks whose structure has been changed by pressure and heat; marble and slate are metamorphic rocks

minerals (MIN-ur-uhls): solid substances that do not come from plants or animals and that make up rocks; copper and aluminum are examples of minerals

sediment (SED-uh-muhnt): bits of rock that break off from larger rocks

sedimentary (sed-uh-MEN-tur-ee): related to rocks formed when layers of sediment are pressed together; limestone and sandstone are sedimentary rocks

silt (silt): fine particles of soil that collect at the bottom of a river or lake

weathering (WETH-ur-ing): the process of being broken down by contact with natural forces such as wind, water, or ice

Thinking Questions

1. What are the three main types of rock?

2. What is lava?

3. How is magma formed?

4. Explain how erosion happens.

5. What forces create metamorphic rock?

Index

Grand Canyon 11

heat 14, 16, 17

igneous rock 5, 7, 8, 16

magma 6, 7, 19

metamorphic rock 5, 16–19

pressure 16–18

sedimentary rock 5, 13, 14, 16

volcano 5, 7

water 8, 10, 11

wind 8, 10

About the Author

A.B. Clamant is the author of several fact-filled books for kids. The daughter of two grade school teachers, she developed a love of children's books at an early age. When she's not writing, she is working on opening her own petting zoo, ABCs Animals. Her favorite foods are bread, fruit strips, and candy. A.B. Clamant lives in Springfield, Missouri, with her four cats: Monkey, Corky, Prissy, and Nelly.